Pet Owner's Guide to the
WEST HIGHLAND WHITE TERRIER

Sheila Cleland

HOWELL
BOOK HOUSE

NEW YORK

HOWELL BOOK HOUSE
A Prentice Hall Macmillan Company
15 Columbus Circle
New York, NY 10023

MACMILLAN is a registered trademark of Macmillan, Inc.

Library of Congress Cataloging-in-Publication data
Cleland, Sheila.
   Pet owner's guide to the West Highland white terrier / Sheila Cleland
   p.   cm.
ISBN 0–87605–921–3
1. West Highland white terriers. I Title
SF429.W4C58   1995
636.7'55 — dc20   95–11924
                                                     CIP

Manufactured in Hong Kong

10 9 8 7 6 5 4 3 2 1

Contents

The West Highland White Terrier, an active little terrier, with a gay, out-going character, is a family favourite worldwide.

About the author

Sheila Cleland has bred, exhibited and judged Westies for some forty years. She has bred nineteen British Champions under her Birkfell prefix and Westies bred by her have become Champions in the USA, Canada, New Zealand, Finland, Sweden, France and Holland. Six Birkfell Westies have won Challenge Certificates at Crufts, including Best of Breed winner Ch. Birkfell Solace. Sheila is in great demand as a Championship show judge. She has judged Crufts and officiated in Sweden, Finland, Denmark, Holland and Germany. She has had the great honour of being invited to judge at the American Terrier Show in Montgomery on two occasions.

Jacket photography: Normhild Sensation, bred and owned by Mrs. D. Lee.

All photographs by Carol Ann Johnson
Unless otherwise credited.

A trio of Birkfell Champions: Ch. Birkfell Student Prince, Ch. Birkfell Samile and Ch. Birkfell Silver Slipper. Anne Roslin-Williams.

Chapter One

CHOOSING A WESTIE

ORIGINS

The West Highland White Terrier originated in the North West of Scotland, and was bred for its working and sporting qualities. The famous Victorian animal painter Sir Edwin Landseer gives proof of this in two of his paintings, dated around 1839. His painting *Sporting Dogs* includes a West Highland White Terrier, and his celebrated *Dignity and Impudence* shows two dogs, one a Bloodhound, the other, "Impudence", unmistakably a Westie.

The original working terriers were used for hunting fox, badger and otter. The main imperative, therefore, was for a small, active dog that could follow its quarry over rough and heathery terrain, and through narrow crevices in the rocks.The value of these little 'earth dogs' is illustrated by a story from the early part of the seventeenth century. King James I of England and VI of Scotland sent a gift of a number of dogs to the King of France, and gave instructions for them to be transported in two different ships, in case one ship foundered.

THE WHITE TERRIER

In the late nineteenth century, white terriers were being separated from their brindle, black and red cousins; these latter developing into Scottish Terriers and Cairn Terriers.

It took a mishap, so the story goes, to break through the custom of destroying any white or lighter-coloured pups. Colonel Malcolm of Poltalloch, Argyllshire, had a favourite reddish-coloured terrier. This dog was accidentally shot when it was mistaken for a fox, so Colonel Malcolm determined to breed white-coloured terriers, which could be more easily recognised.

Having pioneered the breed as working terriers, Colonel Malcolm developed the whites into a distinct strain and type, resembling the modern breed of West Highland White. They were known as Poltalloch Terriers. However, the Cairn Terrier and the Westie continued to be mated together until 1917 in the United States and 1925 in Britain and, even today, there is still a possibility of white hairs in a Cairn and black hairs in a Westie. Small white terriers, known as Roseneath Terriers, were also bred by the Duke of Argyll on his estate at Roseneath. These were reckoned to be of similar breeding to the Poltalloch Terriers, and soon they were grouped together as one breed.

A DISTINCTIVE BREED

The early breeders, especially Colonel Malcolm, emphasised in their writings that the Westie was an active terrier, and must not be allowed to get too broad in front or too wide in the ribs, which would make it difficult to follow the quarry. Meanwhile, the Scottish Terrier was developing into the heavier and broader dog that we see today.

In 1906, the White Terrier exhibitors decided to call their breed the West Highland White Terrier, and breed clubs were formed. Scotland was the pioneer, and, six months later, the West Highland White Terrier Club of England was formed. The breed was exhibited at Crufts in 1907, and it was not long before the new breed caught the imagination of the dog world. By 1908, the first representatives of the new breed were registered with the American Kennel Club - a major breakthrough for the little white terrier from the Highlands of Scotland. For one year only, they were registered as Roseneath Terriers, but in May 1909 the name West Highland White Terrier was adopted, and in the course of the year fourteen dogs and ten bitches were registered with the AKC. In the same year the West Highland Terrier Club of America was established.

THE WAR YEARS

The First World War had a devastating effect on dog breeders as food was in such short supply. Many kennels had to be disbanded, and it was left to a few dedicated Westie enthusiasts to keep the breed alive. Mrs Pacey, one of the very great breeders who produced the famous Wolvey Westies, recalls in her book that a friend was heavily fined by the police for letting her dog finish a rice pudding.

Following the end of the war, the number of kennels was built up again, but all too soon the breed was at risk once more. With the outbreak of the Second World War in 1939, stock from many of the leading kennels had to be dispersed, and some of the most famous dogs were sent to America. This gave a great lift to the breed in North America, but in the UK it was a matter of struggling for survival. Fortunately, a few dogs continued to be registered each year, which was enough to give a nucleus of breeding stock again in 1945. The revival of the breed over the next twenty years was founded on the stock of those who managed to keep the breed going through those difficult years. Mrs Pacey (Wolvey) is remembered along with Dr and Mrs Russell (Cruben), Miss Turnbull (Leal), Miss Wright (Calluna), Miss Wade (Hookwood), Mr and Mrs Beels (Petriburg), Mr and Mrs Dennis (Branston), and Mrs Allom (Furzefield).

THE WESTIE TODAY

As the breed became more firmly established, it found favour in the show ring, but there was not a huge demand from the pet market. However, this was to change in the 1970s when the Westie became increasingly popular, not only in

Cairn Terriers painted by F.T. Daws, reproduced from Hutchinsons Dog Encyclopaedia. The Cairn Terrier and the Westie were mated together until 1925, and you can still get black hairs on a Westie and white hairs on a Cairn.

The Scottish Terrier, 'Ashley Charlie', reproduced from Whinstone's Dogs of Scotland, *published in 1891. The Scottish Terrier is closely related to the Westie, and this picture highlights their common ancestry.*

MR JOHN A. ADAMSON'S SCOTTISH TERRIER "ASHLEY CHARLIE."
Sire, Rambler; Dam, Ashley Moray.

Britain, but also overseas. The demand for quality stock grew rapidly, and many of the UK's top stud dogs went to the United States of America, Scandinavia and Germany.

Today, the Westie is firmly established as one of the most popular pet dogs. In the UK, registrations with the Kennel Club are over 14,000 a year, ranking as the fourth most popular pure-bred dog, and, in the USA, the AKC registers

The Westie was developed as a separate breed, and by 1908, the little terrier from the Highlands of Scotland, had been officially recognised in the USA.

over 10,000 Westies a year. The Westie was brought to public notice by the Best in Show wins at Crufts of Ch. Dianthus Buttons in 1976 and Ch. Olac Moonpilot in 1990. However, there is a danger in excessive popularity, and it is essential that all breed enthusiasts work together to preserve the true Westie type and character.

THE WESTIE CHARACTER

When you consider buying a dog, your first decision must be what size and temperament you want. There are many pictures of pretty, white, small dogs, looking like Westies, which are depicted in advertisements, in books and on television, but these do not convey the character of the breed.

The Westie is first and foremost a terrier, bred to chase and hunt, to work underground out of sight and hearing of its owner, and, therefore, dependent on its own brain and ingenuity. This produces a dog with an independent spirit, an inquisitive nature and an active body.

Some people think that terriers are yappy and snappy. This is not true of a well-brought-up Westie. Although they can be very determined, they do like to please their owners, and so much depends on early training forming a good relationship with your dog. The owner must be prepared to take on the role of 'boss', and as soon as a Westie realises who is 'top of the pack', he will happily do as he is told – though not with the speed and docility of a gundog!

Westies do get on well with children, but I would always be wary of selling a puppy to a family with very small children – unless the parents are experienced dog owners. Puppies and small children are both very demanding, and it is difficult to give both the attention they require. A Westie puppy, aged eight to ten weeks, ready to go to his new home, is very small and vulnerable and could easily be hurt if mishandled – or worse still – dropped. So think carefully before choosing a Westie puppy if you have small children to care for.

PHYSICAL CHARACTERISTICS

Physically, Westies are active and need plenty of exercise. As small dogs, with comparatively short legs, they need the opportunity to run and play. Their intelligent minds mean that they cannot be left alone for long periods of time. Indeed, no dog should be left on its own for hours. This point is one of the most important considerations when deciding to take on a dog. A Westie needs to be brushed and combed regularly. Ideally, this should be on a daily basis, but failing this, you should be prepared to spend time on grooming several times a week. The Westie's coat also needs to be trimmed several times a year. In the majority of cases, pet owners employ the services of a professional dog-groomer for this task. However, for those who wish to show their dog, trimming is a skill to be acquired – and it takes many years to perfect!

MALE OR FEMALE

I do not advise pet owners about whether to have a dog or a bitch, as it is a personal choice. While temperaments are different, they are not so markedly different as in some other breeds. On the whole, Westie males are not so inclined to wander off after in-season bitches, as is the case with many breeds, but they are, or can be, stronger-willed than the bitches (females).

I keep bitches, as I prefer the female temperament, but I must admit that I have had a couple of dogs (males) who were charming characters, and very easy to live with. There is a general belief that bitches are more faithful and more docile, but they can be lively and determined hunters. I have found that my bitches are keener on rabbiting than the dogs. When I had a dog and a couple of bitches in a run with a stone wall on one side, I found that the bitches would climb out of the paddock to go hunting, leaving Fergus running up and down on his own!

However, the female hunting instinct was never more clearly illustrated than on the occasion when my six-year-old champion bitch, Merry, was out for a walk with several other Westies, and she disappeared down an underground tunnel. When she had not surfaced by the next day, we started digging to find the tunnel.

For two days we searched without success. A number of local people were most helpful, and on the fourth evening, a huge mechanical digger arrived to excavate the area. The noise must have driven Merry forwards, and she made her way out of an exit some distance further on, and headed for home, hungry, but none the worse for her adventure!

There is the disadvantage that bitches come into season twice a year. They must be kept away from dogs for about three weeks, and must not be allowed to roam. (But then they should not be roaming on their own at any time!). Bitches can also be more temperamental at this time, but a character change of this sort does not last for long.

If there is any difficulty in keeping dogs away from your bitch when she is in season, and if you have no intention of breeding from her, you can have your bitch spayed (neutered). Nowadays, many people advocate the neutering of all pets, but it is important to remember that spaying is a major operation, and disturbing the balance of hormones can cause side-effects. While these are minimal compared with unwanted litters, nonetheless they can cause complications, such as a change in coat growth, and the possibility of skin problems.

FINDING A BREEDER

When you have definitely decided to buy a puppy, it is advisable to make enquiries to find the names and addresses of several breeders. The secretaries of the breed clubs are a good source of information, as they will be able to give you names and addresses in your area. You should visit the breeders, preferably by appointment, and look at the dogs. Every breeder has his or her own type of Westie, and if you can see several adults, you will be able to form an idea of how the puppies will turn out. You will also see where and how the

LEFT: The Westie is a lively and adaptable dog, and enjoys the company of all members of the family.

BELOW: Puppies should be reared in a clean, fresh environment, and all members of the litter should look healthy, and be lively and out-going in temperament.

Remember the Westie is first and foremost a terrier – a dog with an independent spirit and an inquisitive nature.

The adult Westie, with his sparkling white coat, sturdy little body, and extrovert personality, is an impressive show dog as well as an ideal companion dog.

dogs are kept, whether the kennels are clean, and if the adults have plenty of space, which all make for happier and healthier dogs. Another method of finding the type of Westie you like is to go to one or two Championship dog shows (either all-breed or Specialties). There you will see many Westies, and be able to talk to the breeders who are showing the dogs that appeal to you. You can then make arrangements to go and look at their kennels and their other dogs.

When you have visited several breeders, you will be in a position to decide from which one you want to buy. You should then ask if you can reserve a puppy. There is a great demand for well-reared puppies, so be prepared to wait. At the kennels of your choice you will see the mother of the pups, and, hopefully, some of her relatives. But it is unlikely that the father will be on view, as he often comes from a different, and distant, kennel.

PET OR SHOW
Very often, when I am asked for a puppy, the potential buyer says that they do not want a 'show' pup. However, it should be realised that every litter, bred by an experienced and successful exhibitor, is planned very carefully, with the hope that the litter will contain a top show pup. As no-one can say which, if any, of the litter is show-standard, every puppy is very carefully reared. This makes a good start for every puppy, whether it is to be a much-loved pet or become a top show dog.

ASSESSING THE PUPPIES
If you are hoping to show your Westie, you will have chosen to buy from a winning kennel, and the breeder will give you advice regarding the puppy's potential, as he or she will understand the way the puppies from their breeding usually develop. Hopefully, you will have studied the breed Standard, and will have some idea of what to look for. For my part, the first consideration is what the puppy looks like when he is running about the pen with the rest of the litter. A pup with show potential should catch your eye by the way he carries himself; by the way he holds his head, the balance of his neck and tail, his tail carriage and his overall shape. The general impression is important, as it will catch the judge's eye in the show ring.

The head should be short and broad in muzzle, with a good stop (the point where the muzzle joins the head), because, as the puppy develops, his head will lengthen and the stop will be less obvious. The mouth should be correct at ten weeks, preferably very slightly overshot rather than level. The lower jaw tends to grow on after the top jaw has finished, so that a level mouth at fifteen weeks may well be an undershot mouth at six months. The front legs must be straight and not set too wide apart; the feet should be neat and round. The neck should be long enough to give the puppy 'style' when he moves or stands. Short necks get shorter on maturity. A short, level back is essential, and the body should be deep and rounded at this age. The tail must be well set, and carried well up. It should be short and thick, as a long, thin tail will only get worse. The hindquarters must be broad and rounded. The stifle (the joint of the hindleg, sometimes known as the 'knee') should be well bent, and the hocks (the 'heel' on the hindleg) should be set low. Bone, all through, should be strong.

The coat is very important at this age. The ideal coat is very hard, dense, and almost smooth-looking, with the legs and head showing little of the furnishing (longer hair on the head and legs) that the adult Westie has. Coats with some length can end up being correct. However, a thick, soft coat should be avoided, as it will never grow in hard, no matter how much it is worked on.

At ten weeks, the puppy's ears may not be erect, but you can check the size by turning the puppy on his back to see what he looks like with his ears up. Of course, the pigment should be black on the nose and round the eyes. You should have access to inspect the puppy at six weeks, and at eight to nine weeks – not just the day you are buying him. Remember that even the best dog has his faults, so you should be aware of the faults you can live with, and those you cannot bear. This all comes down to personal preferences, but you must buy a dog you like, as you are going to live with him. It is impossible to pick a puppy and be certain about his future development. When a well-known professional handler was asked at what age you should choose a pup, the answer was "eleven months" – and there is a lot of truth in that.

When your new puppy arrives home, it is the start of a responsibility which will last throughout your Westie's life.

Chapter Two

CARING FOR YOUR PUPPY

PREPARATIONS
Before you collect your puppy, there are preparations to be made to ensure that your puppy's transition to his new home goes as smoothly as possible.

SLEEPING QUARTERS
Where is your puppy going to sleep? This is a far more important decision than you may imagine, as a dog sees his bed as a place of haven where he feels safe and secure. It must therefore be located somewhere that suits both your puppy – and the rest of the household.

Dog beds come in all shapes and sizes, most of which are suitable for Westies. However, it is important to remember that all puppies chew, and it is probably worth waiting a few months before you invest in an expensive bed.

A puppy, and indeed, an adult dog, must be allocated somewhere that is warm, and most importantly of all, draught-free. Many people find that the kitchen or utility room is the most suitable. These rooms usually have the added advantage of having floors that are easy to clean, which is essential during the house-training period. If the kitchen is large enough to fence off a small area, so that the pup has a safe place of his own, so much the better. It will make life easier when working in the kitchen. A child's playpen, lined with wire-mesh or small panels of wire, will serve the purpose well. The floor should be covered with newspaper, and the puppy's bed put inside.

There are many different types of dog beds on the market, but it is advisable to wait until your puppy has grown out of the chewing stage before you invest in a custom-made dog bed. A cardboard box, lined with some soft bedding, will be perfectly adequate for the first few weeks. However, care must be taken that it is not a recycled box, as the glue used on these is poisonous. Wicker baskets, cloth beds or bean bags are not advisable until the puppy is over the chewing stage. Wicker baskets are not good for long-haired dogs, as the hair gets into the mesh of the basket, and it is impossible to clean them satisfactorily. They can also be very dangerous to the dog if they are chewed.

The most resilient is certainly the tough, plastic kidney-shaped dog bed. When a bed of this type is lined with newspaper and soft bedding, it is both comfortable and easy to clean.

DOG CRATES

In the USA it is standard practice to use a dog crate as a bed, and this can be an invaluable item of equipment, if used correctly. The crate should never be viewed by either the dog or the owner as a punishment cell. It provides a safe haven where the puppy can rest undisturbed, and, when lined with soft bedding, it is also a comfortable bed.

A puppy should never be confined to a crate for long periods. Eventually, the puppy will go into the crate of his own free will, regarding it as his special den. Make sure that the dimensions of the crate are suitable for an adult Westie.

Most puppies have been taught by their mothers not to soil their bedding, so always try to give your puppy a bed that he can get out of to relieve himself at night. No small pup will be able to 'go through the night', so he must have access to suitable place, preferably covered in newspaper.

A crate is also a great aid to house-training. No puppy likes to soil his own bed, so if you line one half of the crate with newspaper, the puppy will soon learn to 'be clean' in this area. If this method is used, make sure you buy a large crate. Collapsible crates can also be used in the car, and this is an ideal arrangement as it gives the puppy a safe and secure place for travelling. This will be a great asset in later life.

FEEDING BOWLS

Your Westie will need two bowls, one for food and one for fresh water. A strong, heavy bowl for water should be available for the pup at all times. Do not put too much into it at first, as most puppies love to play with water. I prefer to use dishes made of pottery or stainless steel. I never leave plastic dishes with puppies, as they like to chew almost everything, and plastic is very tempting for them.

You can also buy feeding bowls which are slightly raised off the ground, and these can be useful while your puppy is still small.

COLLAR AND LEAD
Your puppy should be about nine weeks old when you collect him, and he will be too young to start wearing a proper collar and lead. If you feel you must have a lead, a cat collar and lead will serve. I do not like to see small puppies being walked about on leads. Their necks are too delicate, and they can be damaged. Collar and lead training can safely be started at about four months.

TOYS
All puppies chew, especially when they are teething, so it is sensible to provide some toys that the puppy is *allowed* to chew. Toys for puppies are many and varied. They come in all materials and shapes. Select good-quality toys and chew articles that your puppy cannot tear apart or swallow, and do not let him have any old shoes or other human articles. A puppy cannot tell an old shoe from a new one!

GROOMING EQUIPMENT
You should buy a brush and comb so that you can begin grooming your puppy daily. Start with a small wire brush, before graduating to the more effective brushes, which are needed on the thicker coat of the four-month-old puppy.

SAFETY MEASURES
Before you collect your puppy make sure your house and your outdoor area are puppy-proof. The garden should be securely fenced, and any chemicals used for gardening should be safely locked away. In the house, make sure there are no electric wires trailing where the puppy can get at them, and try to ensure that 'chewable' objects are kept out of reach.

COLLECTING YOUR PUPPY
When you are ready to collect your puppy, you should be guided by the breeder as to what time of day is the most suitable. I like people to plan their journey so that they will arrive home with the new puppy no later than late afternoon. This will obviously depend on the distance you have to travel, but if you arrive home in the daytime, it will give the puppy a chance to settle in before he is put to bed for the night.

The journey will be easier if there are two people in the car, even if you have the puppy in a travelling box. The pup will undoubtedly protest loudly, and this

A dog crate is an invaluable item of equipment. It provides comfortable sleeping quarters, and can also be used when travelling in the car.

Your Westie will need a strong, heavy bowl for drinking water, and a feeding bowl. Plastic bowls are not recommended as they can be easily chewed.

Do not rush to start walking your puppy on a lead. Collar and lead training can start at about four months.

can be distracting for the driver. You must take plenty of newspapers and pieces of towelling with you, as the puppy will not have been in a car before, and is likely to be travel-sick. A bottle of water and dish to drink out of will also be useful. Before you leave, there are a number of important items which the breeder should give you. These include:

DIET SHEET: The breeder should have a diet sheet for you, giving accurate details of the food the puppy requires, with times for feeding, and the quantities required. Try to stick to the diet for the first three or four weeks.

PEDIGREE: Among other papers you will receive is your Westie's pedigree. You should examine this, and ask any questions if you are in doubt about any of it. I am disappointed if buyers do not open the pedigree, as it is a history of the puppy, and should be of interest. You may be given the kennel club registration form, signed by the breeder in the transfer section. This should be sent by you to the kennel club to register the puppy in your name. However, sometimes your national form has not come through, in which case it will be sent on to you by the breeder

HEALTH INSURANCE: In the UK it is standard practice among responsible breeders to provide health insurance to cover the first few weeks as the puppy settles into his new home. This is not the case in the USA. When this initial cover runs out, the owner can decide whether to take out an insurance policy for the dog.

ARRIVING HOME
Give your puppy a chance to explore the house and the garden (yard), and introduce members of the family in a calm and controlled manner. This is not an occasion to ask all your friends and neighbours round to admire the new arrival. Your puppy needs a chance to get used to his new surroundings and his new family, before meeting a host of strangers – no matter how well-meaning they are. You can give your puppy a meal, but do not be worried if he seems reluctant to feed. The puppy has so much to get used to as he settles into his new home, he may well experience a temporary loss of appetite. However, most puppies will soon make up for lost time! You may find that your puppy is a bit choosy over food, when there is no competition from his litter-mates, and this is an added reason for sticking to the familiar diet given by the breeder. A different diet is liable to cause stomach upsets, so is best avoided until the puppy is well-established in his new home.

All puppies need plenty of sleep in order to develop strongly. A pup needs a couple of hours sleep during the day. This also serves as a time to train the puppy to be shut away by himself. When a puppy is sound asleep, he should not be woken abruptly. Run a finger gently down his back, or stroke his head. No one likes to be woken up suddenly, and a sudden shock may make your puppy snap at you.

THE FIRST NIGHT
Your new puppy will probably complain loudly when he is first left alone. He will be missing the warmth and company of his brothers and sisters. The ticking of an old alarm clock, wrapped up in a blanket, may well be a comfort to him. However, he will learn to sleep alone if you leave him to cry. If you weaken, and take him up to your bedroom, you will have lost the first battle, and your pup will insist on sleeping in your room for ever after. Of course, if there are neighbours within earshot, you may be forced to capitulate!

HOUSE-TRAINING
Your pup will soon become accustomed to the idea of relieving himself on the newspaper provided for him in his pen. As he grows older, the newspaper can be moved near the door, and then outside.

It pays dividends at this time to spend some time and effort in training your puppy. Most puppies relieve themselves within minutes of having a meal, so you should put your pup outside as soon as he has eaten, on the grass or wherever you want him to go regularly. It is important that you stay out with him until he has done everything necessary, then you should praise him, and bring him back into the house. Even if the weather is cold and wet, you must stay with him and talk to him, repeating some phrase that he will connect with the action. I usually say, "Go and hurry up", and repeat it again when the puppy is actually relieving himself.

Another time when puppies relieve themselves almost immediately is after sleeping. As soon as your puppy wakes up, he should be taken out and encouraged to perform. He will soon learn.

If your pup makes a mistake in the house, you should pick him up and scold him, using your voice to indicate your displeasure. Then put him out in the usual place, again using your customary phrase. Be sure to mop up the puddle thoroughly, and wash the carpet or floor with a suitable carpet shampoo. There are good foam shampoos that you can spray on and wipe off. It is important to remove all scent of the mistake, so that your puppy does not get into the habit of soiling the house.

FEEDING REGIME
The diet I recommend for puppies is:

8am: Cereal (porridge, semolina or cornflakes) with milk or a good-quality puppy meal with milk or warm water.
Noon: Raw, lean, chopped beef with some plain wholemeal puppy meal or stale brown bread.
5pm: Same as noon with some calcium supplement.
Bedtime: Same as breakfast.
(Some people feed scrambled eggs as a protein meal. However, my puppies have always been sick almost immediately when eating this, so now I never feed anything containing egg.)

After you have followed the breeder's diet sheet for a few weeks, you can start to change it, if you wish to do so, but make sure you do this gradually. Any sudden change of diet can cause diarrhoea, so the best course of action is to mix the new food in with the normal diet, which gives the puppy's metabolism a chance to adapt to the change.

If your puppy develops diarrhoea, reduce quantities of food, and give boiled rice with chicken. Reduce the quantity of milk, or give semi-skimmed milk with cornmeal. (Make sure the puppy has access to fresh water to keep his fluid levels up.)

As long as the puppy is still lively, do not worry too much for a day or two. However, if after two days on a light diet, the diarrhoea persists, consult your

Your puppy will need two meat and two cereal meals a day to start with.

It is a good idea to provide rawhide chews to get your puppy through the teething stage.

vet. A puppy is very small and must not be allowed to become dehydrated.

Another potential problem with a puppy leaving the litter is that there is no competition for the food, and some puppies seem to lose interest in one or all of their meals. The first couple of times that this happens, the food should be taken away after five – but not more than ten – minutes. If you find there is one particular food that your puppy does not like, replace it with something different at the next meal. Do not take away one kind of food and immediately offer another kind. Your pup will soon learn to take advantage of you, and will try to manipulate you again.

Once again, it must be stressed that as long as your puppy is well and lively, there is nothing to worry about. The minute your pup seems listless or off-colour, you should seek professional assistance. Happily, this is an unlikely happening in a hardy breed such as the Westie.

INOCULATIONS

Before you collect your puppy, it is advisable to contact your vet to ask him the age he considers it best to start your puppy's inoculations. The age varies, as there are different brands of vaccine, and the conditions in different areas must be taken into consideration. The usual system is for the first inoculation to be given at ten weeks, with a second one two weeks later. In some areas, a final inoculation for parvovirus is advised at eighteen weeks.

The diseases covered by inoculation include distemper, once a real scourge for the dog, but no longer so. Now, thanks to many years of effective vaccination, this disease is much less common. Other diseases covered are leptospirosis, canine hepatitis and parvovirus. Parvovirus came into prominence some fifteen years ago, and killed thousands of dogs. The virus is carried on clothes or shoes, and takes hold of a pup very quickly. It is essential with this vaccine that the antibodies from the mother, which are passed through to the puppy, are no longer in the puppy's system, or the vaccine will have no effect. This is the reason that some vets like to give a third injection at eighteen weeks.

In most cases, the inoculations have no adverse effect on the pup. Occasionally, a puppy can be off-colour for a few days after the injection. If the effects last more than a day, contact your vet, and ask his advice. Very occasionally, as with any inoculation, there can be serious side effects. Between the two injections, and for two weeks after the second injection, the puppy should be kept at home, and stay reasonably quiet. Care should be taken that there is no contact with dogs that are not fully inoculated until the vaccine has had a chance to take effect.

WORMING

Virtually all puppies carry a burden of roundworm, despite worming the bitch prior to mating, and no matter how well the puppies are reared. Your puppy's breeder will inform you of the worming programme already adopted. My puppies are wormed at about three weeks and five weeks. Occasionally, I will give another dose at eight weeks. After that, I give a dose at four and a half months. Nowadays, there is great concern about worms, and some vets advocate very frequent worm doses. You must, of course, be advised by your own vet, but too many worm doses can do more damage than not worming at all. The symptoms of worm infestation in a dog are a dry, rough coat, slightly running eyes, vomiting or passing the occasional worm. Pet shops stock worm pills, but it is advisable to seek advice from your vet on the most suitable type to use and the dosage.

SOCIAL TRAINING

When your puppy is fully inoculated, you should start introducing him to other people and dogs. This must be done carefully, so that there is no danger of frightening him. It is better if introductions take place in your house or garden, where your pup is in familiar surroundings. Encourage your friends to stroke and play with your puppy, so that he gets used to being handled by strangers.

Westie puppies often like to chew gently on your fingers when playing, which is just a sign of affection. However, if your puppy snaps or loses his temper, he should be scolded right away. He should never be allowed, even when small, to snap in anger. Reprimand your pup, and afterwards ask yourself what happened to cause the situation. It could be that you did something to provoke him, and you must realise that it was your mistake. Even so, always scold your pup as soon as he shows temper, and wait until afterwards to analyse the event.

Let your puppy run around freely when you are playing with him. Many people like to pick up and cuddle a puppy. It must be remembered that a puppy wriggles when picked up, and it is very easy to drop it and risk serious injury. Discourage your friends, and particularly youngsters, from lifting your pup. As likely as not, he will soon get bored with being held, and want to run about again.

Puppies are like babies and need a lot of sleep. I have found that the puppies I keep develop stronger bone and better condition than their littermates that have gone as pets. I have come to the conclusion that my pups get more undisturbed sleep, when they want it during the day, than a pup living in a busy household. It is a good practice to shut your puppy in a quiet place by himself for a couple of hours in the middle of the day. It will give him a good rest, and also teach him to stay alone in a room.

During the rest of the day, you will find your pup playing hard, then falling quite suddenly into a deep sleep. If possible, let him sleep. If you must wake him, touch him gently by running a finger down his back, so that he is not startled.

Establishing a good relationship with your Westie is the key to achieving basic control and obedience.

Chapter Three

TRAINING

THE RIGHT START

You should start to train a puppy as soon as you get him. If you have bought your Westie from an experienced breeder, the puppy should already be used to being handled; being picked up, being stood on a table, and being brushed. From then on, it is up to you!

Much of the early training of your puppy does not take the form of formal lessons. Talk to your puppy, and he will soon learn from the tone of your voice when you are pleased with him, and when you are not pleased. I believe that most of the correction that you give your dog should be in your voice, but a mild shake may be necessary if your puppy is defiant. Most Westies are anxious to please, and if the first shake is definite enough, and accompanied by a loud, firm "No", you may never have to shake him again.

When your puppy is about four months old, he may decide to try to take over, and will snap at you. He may try this on when you are brushing him, or taking a toy away. This is something that you must *never* let your puppy get away with. He must be firmly corrected or he will think he is winning, and the next time he will bite harder. You will quickly learn the difference between bad-tempered snapping, when your puppy bristles up with anger – which requires immediate disciplinary action – and a playful mouthing of your hand, when the puppy is wagging his tail and is full of fun.

TRAINING TARGETS

The Westie is a bright, intelligent dog, and is capable of reaching a high level of understanding. However, we are talking about a terrier, with a terrier's typical independent spirit, so you must adapt your training methods to suit your dog. Most Westies enjoy human companionship, and they aim to please, so there is no reason why you cannot achieve a good level of basic Obedience. In fact, this is a minimum requirement if you are to have an adaptable companion that you can take out with you, confident that he will respond in a calm and controlled manner in most situations.

SAYING "NO"

The most useful word to teach your puppy is "No". It is short and sharp, and can cover any eventuality. If your pup gets hold of something, or is chewing a forbidden object, it is essential that he learns to respond immediately to a firm "No". When the puppy responds, you must give him plenty of praise. At the beginning of training, it is a good idea to exaggerate your praise. If you sound pleased and happy as you say "Good Boy", and give a cuddle at the same time, the puppy will soon understand that you are pleased. Later, a pat will do, but at first it is better to be effusive in your praise.

HOUSE RULES
Do not let your puppy jump on the furniture or rush up and down stairs. It is very bad for the joints of a growing puppy (see Legge-Perthes disease, Chapter Seven). A firm "No" right from the start is easier than trying to break an established habit.

TRAVELLING
In most cases, the puppy's first trips in the car will be to the vet. Try to make car journeys end in a short walk, or some pleasurable outing, driving only a few miles at a time. Make sure that the puppy has fully relieved himself before starting out on any car journey, and avoid feeding just before an outing. The puppy can either sit on the passenger's lap or be put in a good-quality travelling box. Cover the car seats or passenger's lap, as the puppy will very likely be sick until he gets used to the car. Do not let a young pup wander about the car. This will almost certainly cause sickness, and he may hurt himself.

NOISE
Many people say that terriers are yappers, but there is no need for a dog to bark without a reason. You should discourage your puppy from barking too much by using the word "No". Start when the pup is young, so that barking does not become a habit. If he persists when you have told him to stop, get hold of him firmly and give him a shake while repeating "No". Once again, praise him when he is quiet.

It is a good idea to teach your puppy to be left in a room by himself. Start this exercise while your Westie is still young, so that he gets used to going to his bed to rest for an hour or two every day. Most puppies soon get tired of complaining – so do not give in if your puppy starts off by making a fuss.

When your Westie is older, he will almost certainly develop a protective attitude to his house, and will bark when there are strangers about. You will then detect a different type of bark, which serves as a warning.

It is important to train your dog to be adaptable. Once he is house-trained, move his bed to different rooms, and even out into the garage, so that he will learn to settle wherever you put his bed.

COMING WHEN CALLED
The moment you collect your puppy, start using his name on all occasions. It is

amazing how quickly a Westie learns, particularly if his name is connected with pleasurable things, such as being given a cuddle or a plate of food.

The name can then be connected with the command "Come", which should be among the earliest words you teach your pup. Small puppies run willingly to their owners, especially if you squat down to their level. The breeder may well have already started this exercise by calling the puppies at mealtimes.

When you call your puppy and he comes to you, he should be praised lavishly. As your Westie gets older, usually at around five or six months, he will probably realise that he is quicker than you, and will start to run rings around you. A few small pieces of biscuit, kept in your pocket as a reward for coming, are invaluable at such a time. If the pup is sniffing about and not paying attention to you, call his name sharply before calling "Come". Then, be sure to reward him when he comes.

SIT
This is a useful exercise for pet puppies, but a future show puppy should be taught the Stand instead, as this is what will be required in the show ring. The usual way to teach the Sit is to gently push the puppy's hindquarters down while holding a tidbit over the pup's head, making him lift his head back. When the puppy sits, he should be given a tidbit and praised. Gradually lengthen the period you keep your puppy in the Sit position, until he learns to stay until he is called.

STAND
Show dogs, or potential show dogs, should not be taught to sit for a treat. In the show ring you will require your dog to stand with head and tail up, ears pricked, looking for a tidbit, so if a dog has been taught the Sit, you may have problems. My show dogs are never taught the command "Sit", but much the same control can be exercised if the dog is taught the command "Stand".

DOWN
The Down is a natural extension of the Sit. You need to start with your puppy in the Sit, and holding a tidbit, drop your hand to ground level. The puppy will go into the Down in order to get at the tidbit, and this is when you should give the command "Down" followed by the reward, and plenty of praise. When training on the lead, the exercise can be taught giving a downward tug on the lead, and applying light pressure on the forequarters.

STAY
The Stay is useful in a variety of different situations, and should be among the early lessons that you teach your puppy. It can be taught in conjunction with the Sit and the Down, or if you are showing your puppy, the Stand. It is best to teach this exercise with your puppy on the lead, so that you remain in control. If a puppy gets the exercise correct from the beginning, he will quickly

The Sit exercise can be taught using tidbits, then you can graduate to giving the command and applying light pressure on the hindquarters.

The Down is a natural extension of teaching the Sit. Again, your Westie will learn quickly if you use tidbits.

The Stay is a very useful exercise, which comes in handy in a variety of situations. Build up distances gradually, so that your Westie does not feel insecure.

associate the command with the right action. If a puppy keeps breaking the Stay, you could be in for all sorts of trouble.

This is an exercise where you should progress a little at a time, gradually extending the distance that you leave your puppy. The command, reinforced with a hand signal, helps the pup to understand what is required. Do not forget to give plenty of praise when your puppy responds correctly.

LEAD TRAINING
Put a light collar on your puppy when he is about three and a half months old. When he is comfortable with that, attach a lead, and let him trail it about for a short time, making sure he does not get tangled up. When your pup is accustomed to this, take him out on to the grass, and follow him about, holding the end of the lead. After a minute or two, put a little pressure on the lead, and encourage your puppy to come to you. Then walk slowly with the puppy at your side.

At first, your puppy may throw himself about like a fish on a line, which is the reason you must start on a soft surface. While he is jumping around, bend down and encourage him to come to you, and pat him when he does. Keep these training sessions short, with the puppy on the lead for a few minutes at a time, and finish the lesson when he comes to you. Most puppies learn quite quickly not to fight the lead.

Teach your puppy to walk without pulling by talking to him and encouraging him to stay by your side. Pull him back every time he goes too far forward. Do not put him on an extending lead until he walks well on an ordinary lead.

If you intend showing your puppy, teach him to walk on a lead on either side of you. Although it is customary to walk your dog on the left-hand side, a dog in the ring may have to walk on either side, so it is important that your dog learns to be adaptable.

TRAINING CLASSES
Many dog clubs also run classes for show training. Even if you do not want to show your Westie, this is an opportunity for your pup to meet other dogs, and to be handled by experienced people. Five to six months is young enough to start. A good Obedience training class is an even better option. Go and watch a class before you enrol, and see how the instructor handles the dogs. Some instructors can be too rough with small dogs, and although firm control is necessary, it should be tempered with an understanding of the individual dogs.

THE GOOD CITIZEN SCHEME
The national Kennel Clubs in the UK and in the US have both introduced Good Citizen schemes to encourage a responsible attitude towards dog ownership. The aim is for the dog to be trained to complete a number of simple exercises, aimed at producing a well-mannered, well-socialised dog who will fit in well with the community.

UNITED STATES
The exercises include:
1. Accepting a friendly stranger: To demonstrate that the dog will allow a friendly stranger to approach and speak to the handler in a natural everyday situation.
2. Sitting politely for petting: To demonstrate that the dog will allow a friendly stranger to touch him while he is out with his handler.
3. Appearance and grooming: To demonstrate that the dog will welcome being groomed and examined and will permit a stranger to do so.
4. Out for a walk with the dog on a loose leash: To demonstrate that the handler is in charge of the dog.
5. Walking through a crowd: To demonstrate that the dog can move about politely in pedestrian places and is under control in public places.
6. Sit and Down on command/Staying in place: To demonstrate that the dog will respond to the handler's commands "Sit" and "Down", and will remain in the place commanded by the handler.
7. Praise/interaction: To demonstrate that the dog can be easily calmed following play or praise.
8. Reaction to another dog: To demonstrate that the dog can behave politely around other dogs.
9. Reaction to distractions: To demonstrate that the dog is confident at all times when faced with common distracting situations.
10. Supervised isolation: To demonstrate that a dog can be left alone, if necessary.

BRITAIN
The exercises include:
1. Putting your dog on a collar and lead.
2. The dog must walk on a lead without distraction; the dog should walk steadily on the left side of the handler.
3. The dog and handler must walk through a door or gate.
4. The dog must be on a lead and ignore other dogs and people, walking quietly while the handler holds a conversation for one minute.
5. The dog, with lead attached, must be left by the handler for one minute at a distance of five metres – the handler remains in sight.
6. The dog must stand steady while being groomed.
7. The handler presents the dog on lead for examination, and the examination includes mouth, teeth, throat, eyes, ears and feet.
8. The handler releases the dog from the lead, the dog is allowed to play, and is then recalled and the lead attached.

MINI-AGILITY
For the fit and active, this sport is great fun – and the dogs really seem to enjoy it. There is a special mini-agility course for smaller dogs where they can tackle

With lead training, the aim is to teach your Westie to walk by your side, neither pulling forward nor dragging behind.

If you are planning to show your Westie, you will have to teach the puppy to walk on the left handside, and the right handside.

With good socialisation and training, your Westie will learn to adapt calmly and happily to a variety of different situations. Anne Roslin-Williams.

all the obstacles, but with the height adjusted for their size. It is not as easy as it looks, and it requires a fair degree of training and control to compete in this sport. The obstacles to be negotiated usually include: hurdles, a tunnel, a long jump, an A-frame, a see-saw, and a walkway.

THERAPY DOGS

This is something that any Westie owner can be involved in, so long as their dog is well-mannered and well-socialised. Schemes are run so that dogs can visit patients in hospitals and residents in homes for the elderly. The aim is to comfort those who can no longer keep a dog, and the Westie with its extrovert character, is an ideal candidate for this type of work.

Chapter Four

ADULT MAINTENANCE

FEEDING
There are a great many ways of feeding dogs. New dog foods, all apparently perfectly balanced for every dog, appear each month, and each brings its own advice. For the pet owner, the method you adopt is largely a matter of personal choice and convenience. The basic methods of feeding are as follows:

FRESH/FROZEN MEAT AND BISCUITS
There are many frozen meats that can be obtained from pet shops, butchers' shops and supermarkets. Lean mince (chopped beef) or offal (organ meats) is good for your dog, and can be fed raw. Chicken and rabbit must be cooked. Some dogs find one type of meat more palatable than another, and it is important that your dog should enjoy his food.

As regards quantity, about three ounces of meat, once a day, is sufficient for a Westie. This should be mixed with an equal quantity of wholemeal biscuit meal or brown bread.

It is worth taking time to enquire about the meal or mixer. Some are deep-fried to make them more palatable, but these should be avoided as they are too fattening. I use one that is advertised as having 'no additives', so that if I want my dogs to have extra vitamins and minerals, I can provide them myself.

The meat and biscuit diet is considered by some to be out of date, but it has served dog breeders for generations. However, it does need a little more thought and effort than some of the other methods.

CANNED FOODS
There are many different canned foods available. A few are complete diets and should, therefore, be fed on their own. The majority are meats and are designed to be fed with an equal quantity of meal or bread. Always choose a good-quality brand of canned food; the cheaper brands contain a lot of jelly or gravy.

I always choose canned food containing white meats, such as chicken, turkey or rabbit, as I feel this suits a Westie's metabolism better than beef. I never feed cans with liver or heart.

Although manufacturers give suggested quantities on the label, this

Your Westie needs regular grooming, and this is also a good time to check your dog's general health and condition.

ABOVE: Teeth can be kept clean, using canine toothpaste and a toothbrush.

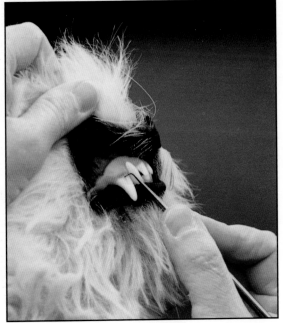

LEFT: If tartar accumulates on the teeth, this may need to be scraped off.

information should be treated with caution. Three or four ounces a day is enough for a Westie, with an equal quantity of meal. One well-known manufacturer recommended on the label the incredible amount of thirteen ounces of meat a day. This excessive amount would almost certainly result in diarrhoea, skin trouble and obesity.

DRIED FOODS

Over the last fifteen years, there has been an enormous growth of dried dog foods on the market. Some take the form of flaked food, and many are in pellet form. These are all complete foods, and should not have meat scraps or any other supplements added, as this will spoil the balance. The manufacturer's instructions must be followed, as some foods are soaked and others fed dry. It is absolutely essential that plenty of fresh water is available at all times. Although this is necessary with whatever is fed, it is especially important with dried food.

Over many years, I have found the best system of feeding Westie adults is to give a very hard, dry biscuit at midday, and to give the main meal at night. This consists of three to four ounces of raw or cooked tripe or meat, with a good handful of soaked meal.

Care should be taken not to give tidbits too often. Dogs should never be fed while you are eating, because they can become very demanding. Ideally, the rule is: 'No treats at all!' But a total ban is difficult to enforce. The most important point to bear in mind is that obesity leads to a multitude of health problems, and so it is unfair to your dog to allow him to become overweight.

EXERCISE

All dogs need exercise, even when they are still small. However, you have to build up a routine of daily exercise gradually, as a puppy is very vulnerable while it is still growing.

Small pups should be allowed to play outside whenever the weather is reasonable. The puppy should not be lead-trained too soon, but by five months he could be trained, and ready for short walks. Your Westie should not be walked far on the lead until he is eight or nine months, but short walks among strangers and traffic will educate him to new sights and sounds.

Free running about in a garden or larger enclosed area is a great help in developing muscles. When he is fully grown, a Westie should have plenty of fresh air, time to play in the garden, and a good, brisk walk every day. The walk is valuable as much for the dog's mental development as for the physical benefits.

HEALTH CHECKS

It is important to keep a regular check on your Westie's general health and condition, because if problems are spotted at an early stage, they are much easier to treat. The best time to do this is when you are grooming, which should be a procedure carried out on a routine basis.

TEETH AND GUMS

Your Westie will probably start teething – losing his milk teeth – from around four months of age. You will want to check which puppy teeth are loose or have fallen out, and how the new ones are coming on. Therefore, it is important to get your puppy used to being handled in this way from an early age. Be careful when your puppy is actually teething, as the gums can be very sore at this time.

As he grows, you will be able to monitor the condition of gums and teeth. The teeth must be kept clean and free of tartar. If this is allowed to accumulate the teeth become discoloured, the dog's breath may smell and it may even lead to an infection of the gums. Usually, tartar is kept at bay if your Westie is given hard biscuits to chew on. An occasional bone – the nylabone type is ideal – will also help to keep the teeth clean.

If tartar does accumulate, you will have to clean the teeth. This can be done using a canine toothpaste and toothbrush. Most Westies soon get used to this procedure. In more severe cases, you will need to scrape the teeth clean. If you are unsure of how to do this, ask your vet to show you how.

EYES

Next, look at eyes to make sure that there is no discharge. Most dogs collect dry dust particles or 'sleep' at the corners of the eyes, and this should be removed daily. You should seek professional advice if there is any evidence of caking or runny eyes.

EARS

The condition of the ears should be checked when grooming. Often, when the ear is sore, the dog will hold its head tilted to one side. There could be an unpleasant smell, indicating that all is not well. If this is the case, you should consult your veterinary surgeon and get some suitable drops. Follow the directions carefully for a week, and if there is not a noticeable improvement, go back for a different medication. There are many causes of ear problems, from fungal infection to mites, all of which used to come under the general term of 'canker'. Nowadays, there is a varied selection of ear-drops and ointments to deal with these common problems.

NAILS

A regular check should be made on the toenails, especially the dewclaws. Dewclaws are found on the front legs, about an inch above the foot, and occasionally on the hind legs as well. Some breeders remove them when the puppies are only a few days old, so you will need to check to see if your pup has them. Dew-claw nails are not in a position to be worn down, and often

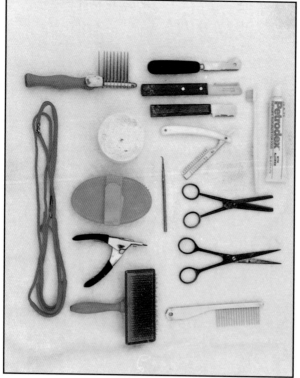

ABOVE: If nails are not worn down naturally, they will need to be trimmed, using nail-clippers.

LEFT: Grooming kit for a show Westie. This includes a brush and comb, a slicker pad, nail-clippers, canine toothpaste and toothbrush, chalk, scissors, a variety of stripping tools, and a show lead.

This puppy is having his first hand-strip. This is a process when the old, dead hair is plucked out, using finger and thumb.

This Westie puppy has been hand-stripped, and the new coat will start to come through.

grow in a circle. If they are left untrimmed, they will grow into the leg, causing considerable pain.

Generally, if a dog is given sufficient exercise on hard surfaces, the toenails should not grow too long, but, in some situations, this is not possible. If nails are allowed to grow long, the quick, which can be seen as a pink line in white nails (it is not visible in black nails), also grows longer. It therefore becomes impossible to cut the nails back as short as they should be, and gradually the whole foot will go out of shape. If you want to trim your dog's nails yourself, you will need to buy a guillotine type nail-clipper. Great care should be taken not to cut back too far, for, if you cut into the quick, it will bleed profusely and will cause the dog considerable pain. Most professional dog groomers cut the nails as part of the service. If this is not the case, you could ask your vet to cut the nails and show you how to do it yourself.

THE VETERAN WESTIE
Fortunately, the Westie is a hardy, no-nonsense breed, and, with luck, your Westie will live to a ripe old age. However, needs change as a dog grows older, and you should be ready to adapt to your dog's particular requirements.

Commonsense should govern the amount of exercise given as the dog grows old. At the age of twelve or so, the veteran dog should be allowed to go for shorter walks, and to move at his own pace. All dogs are individuals, so you should judge according to your own dog's needs. Some dogs will thrive on exercise, particularly if they are in the company of a younger dog, others are quite content to take things easy.

You may need to make some changes to diet as your dog gets older. If the teeth are not as good as they were, you may need to cut down on the amount of biscuit you feed. Some elderly dogs prefer to have their main meal split into smaller meals, as they find smaller amounts are easier to digest. Again, this depends on the individual dog.

An old dog likes his comfort, so make sure your veteran Westie is never allowed to get cold and wet. His bed should be located somewhere warm and draught-free, and he should be allowed periods where he can rest undisturbed. If you have a younger dog in the house, make sure the 'oldie' does not feel left out. A dog who has done everything ever asked of him over the years deserves your best care and attention.

It is essential to keep the veteran Westie well-groomed, and trimmed. This not only makes the dog more comfortable, it also ensures that you are keeping a regular check on the overall condition when you are grooming. Early diagnosis of health problems can save much suffering and pain.

Finally, when your Westie is failing in health and losing his quality of life, do not balk at making the decision to put him to sleep, if this is what the vet recommends. It is never an easy decision to make, but you owe it to your pet to give him a dignified exit from the world, and to save him from any further suffering.

GROOMING
START AS YOU MEAN TO GO ON
Ideally, the Westie's coat consists of a hard, straight outer-coat, and a thick, short, soft undercoat. In fact, coats vary tremendously, depending on breeding and environment. Sometimes, the top coat is soft and wavy, and sometimes, there is no undercoat. All types of coat must be brushed and combed regularly. If this is done daily, it will only take a few minutes each time.

GROOMING YOUR PUPPY
While your puppy is still small, stand him on a table or some other non-slippery surface of similar height. You may find it helpful to place a rubber mat on the table to ensure that your puppy does not slip.

To start with, use a small, moderately stiff brush. The first stage is to brush gently from tail to head, brushing the hair up. Then brush the coat flat from head to tail. Take special notice of the tummy and the insides of the legs, where the hair is most likely to become matted.

When your puppy is very young, this routine is really a matter of training, so that your Westie will learn to enjoy the attention. Although some pups may wriggle and resist to start with, most soon learn to stand quietly. The great advantage of starting grooming at this early stage is that when your Westie is old enough to need fuller grooming, he will understand the routine.

As the puppy's coat grows, change your brush to a wire, slicker type brush, and you will also need a steel comb with fairly widely-spaced teeth. The dog should be thoroughly brushed, as before, using the slicker, and then combed to ensure that there is no matted hair anywhere. If you find a small tangle, do not pull the comb roughly through the hair, but try to brush it out. If the mat is in a sensitive place, on the inside of the leg or tummy, cut the tangle out. The hair on the head should first be brushed back from the face, then combed or brushed upwards to give the 'woolly' look.

TRIMMING
The Westie sheds his undercoat twice a year, and the topcoat is shed gradually as it dies. The coat, therefore, must be trimmed regularly to keep it in good condition. The undercoat must be brushed out thoroughly when shedding, because it will get very matted if it gets wet or when it is washed, when the short, soft hairs are loose in the longer topcoat.

Trimming is a skilled job, and it takes a long time and a lot of experience to turn out a smart-looking Westie. Show exhibitors spend many years watching and learning from the more experienced breeders, so that they present their dog to his best advantage. The average pet owner will not want to undertake so complicated a project.

In order to keep your pet Westie in good condition, you will need to make enquiries in your area to locate a professional dog groomer. Do try to find someone who is experienced in trimming Westies.

*An adult
Westie ready
for hand-
stripping,
clipping and
grooming.*

*Hand-stripping
should be done,
a little at a time,
every few days.*

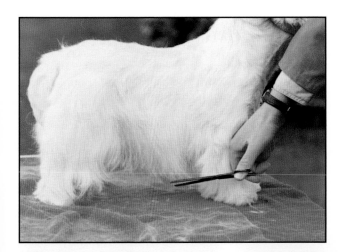

The length of the coat is trimmed.

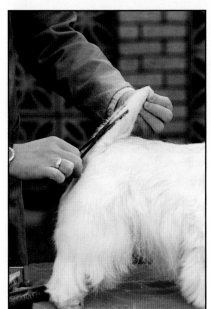

The tail is trimmed so that it has the typical 'carrot' shape, tapering to a point.

The hair is trimmed round the neck. It is important to trim a little at a time, so that the coat blends evenly from one area to another.

HAND-STRIPPING

A good-quality coat will grow to a length of 2.5 inches or more, and by then it will be very untidy and dead-looking. At this point the coat pulls out quite easily, a few hairs at a time. Hand-stripping, when done correctly, means pulling the hair, using finger and thumb. Nowadays, many people use a stripping knife, but the finger and thumb method is the traditional, tried and trusted way.

The hair is pulled from the back of the head towards the tail. This is a job that can only really be tackled by the owner, as it should be done, a little at a time, when the coat is loose, otherwise it is painful for the dog. The professional groomer, who advertises hand-stripping, will need to have the dog back every eight to ten weeks. Thinning scissors must be used in the more sensitive areas.

CLIPPING

For many years, clipping was considered bad for terriers. Nowadays, many terriers are clipped satisfactorily, and look very smart. This process involves using electric clippers, and gives a nice, neat appearance to the pet dog, as long as he is not clipped too close. A Westie should be clipped at least three times a year.

Show dogs should not have clippers used on them, as a short coat must be shaped to lie correctly over many months, and a variety of tools are used to get the right effect.

BATHING

Many groomers wash the dog after trimming, but most Westies are quite clean when the outer-coat is removed. I have never believed in washing dogs, and, indeed, I have known many breeders who never even washed their show dogs. Instead, they used a dry-cleaning powder, as they felt that soap and water spoiled the texture of the coat.

Although I do wash my show dogs, I do not wash the dogs I trim, unless the owners particularly ask for this. The more a Westie coat is washed, the more quickly it seems to get dirty. Regular brushing is the secret to a clean coat. If your dog is very dirty after a walk, or, in the case of a male, gets smelly underneath, he can be stood in tepid water and rinsed off.

STEP-BY-STEP GUIDE TO TRIMMING

Trimming for show has to be done over a long period. It is necessary to build up the coat gradually to give the correct length and shape of hair in time for the show season. It is easier to see results if you trim for a short time every day or so, and then see how it looks when your dog is running about.

The first thing to do is to assess your dog's faults and virtues. The art of trimming is to hide the faults and enhance the virtues – and make the whole thing look natural.

THE BODY

Start by getting the hair on the neck and the back in condition., Rub some chalk (calcium carbonate) on to your fingers and on to the dog's coat. This improves the hold you get on the hair, in order to pull it. Brush the coat up and then flat, and, starting from the neck, pull out the longest hairs, a few at a time. The hair must be pulled the way the hair grows, i.e. towards the tail. If the hair does not come easily, it is not dead, and therefore not ready to come out.

If you simply need to shorten the coat, and not take any out, you should use a trimming knife. The aim is to blend the neck into the back, and then make the back level. Shape the coat, in the same way, down the sides and on the body. Try not to make holes in the coat, as you will then have to trim down to make it even. Again, the secret is to do a little at a time.

The hair on the quarters should be thicker and longer than the hair on the back, with the hair being tapered to fit.

THE TAIL

The hair on the upper side of the tail must be tidied up by pulling out the long, wispy hair. Be careful not to take too much off, as there is nearly always a patch, an inch or so from the root of the tail, where the hair is thinner than the rest.

Next, trim the sides of the tail, either pulling the hair out or using thinning scissors, tapering the hair towards the tip of the tail. The underside of the tail can be done with straight scissors or thinning scissors. Trim up the tail from root to tip.

Be careful how much hair you take off where the tail joins the body. Incorrect trimming here can ruin the topline, making the tail appear low-set, or the quarters appear incorrect.

THE HINDQUARTERS

The next step is to trim down the rear end, using straight scissors or thinning scissors. Take the hair very close under the tail, tapering towards the quarters.

THE FOREQUARTERS

Using thinning scissors, trim up the chest and neck, with the scissors pointing up towards throat. Continue with the thinning scissors under the jaw, to a point about an inch from the chin, and sideways to the ear. The jaw-line is the guide. Trim under the jaw, but not above it.

Thin out the hair on the shoulders, from the ear to the top of the foreleg. Do not take it very close, so that you can finish it with a knife or with finger and thumb, and blend it into the longer hair on the neck and body.

Leave the hair at the base of the breastbone a little longer than at the chest, and leave plenty of hair at the top of the legs, when viewed from the front.

Brush the hair on the front legs up and then smooth down. Pull out the

The feet are tidied up to give the desired, neat appearance.

The coat is combed through thoroughly.

A brush is used to fluff up the coat on the legs. The coat on the head also needs fluffing up.

The finished product, looking immaculate with a beautifully trimmed coat.

longest hairs, so that the leg is thick and even. Make sure that, when viewed from the front, the hair on the elbows does not stick out to make your Westie look bandy-legged.

THE FEET

Trim the feet with straight scissors. First, trim from the underside of the foot, cutting away as much as possible between the pads. Then, holding one front foot up, trim around the other front foot. Do the same with the other front foot. Trim the hind feet in the same way.

Trim the inside of the hindlegs with the thinning scissors, shortening the long hairs, a little at a time, until the required shape is achieved. Make sure that the toenails are kept trimmed. trim the hair under the body by shaping with thinning scissors.

THE HEAD

Trim the head last so that the overall balance can be maintained. Brush the head up, and then trim the top two-thirds of the ears. Rub chalk on to the ears, and on to your fingers, and pull out a few hairs at a time until you have a smooth, velvety appearance on both sides of the ear. If you must use scissors on the edges of the ear, always cut up towards the tip. However, great care must be taken, as ears bleed very easily from the smallest nick, and it can take quite a time to stop.

Next, finish the head by trimming the ends of the hair with thinning scissors. Keep brushing the hair up frequently, so that the shape can be seen. Be careful to take only a very little off at a time.

Having trimmed your Westie into shape, you must be sure to improve the outline by brushing every two or three days, and removing the stray, dead hairs that constantly appear.

Chapter Five

SHOWING YOUR WESTIE

Showing dogs is a great hobby, but it is not one to embark on without careful thought and consideration. It involves quite a lot of expense, much hard work, and total dedication. If you are interested in showing your Westie, the best course of action is to find out where local shows are being held. Go along to a show or two, talk to Westie exhibitors and watch the proceedings. Championship shows are different from the smaller shows, and it depends on your temperament as to which you prefer. Rules and regulations for showing dogs vary from country to country, but the same broad principles apply as regards handling dogs in the show ring and judging the breed.

BRITAIN
Kennel Club Shows are basically divided into three categories:

ALL BREED CHAMPIONSHIP SHOWS
These are large shows usually held over two or three days. There are about thirty of these during the year, often held out of doors, with different groups of dogs competing on different days. Most of the breeds with classes at these shows have Kennel Club Challenge Certificates on offer. Challenge Certificates are awarded to the best dog and the best bitch in the breed.

To earn the title of Champion, the dog or bitch must win three Challenge Certificates (CCs) under three different judges. The competition at Championship Shows is intense, and exhibitors are very keen to win the treasured CCs. These shows also provide a meeting point for breeders from all corners of the country, and provide good opportunities to make friends, discuss problems, and to see the cream of a breed.

BREED CLUB SHOWS (Championship and Open)
At the Championship Show, certificates are on offer as at the All Breed Shows; but the atmosphere is more relaxed, because they are catering for only one breed. The distance from car to show ring is much less, and there is more time and opportunity for talking to breeders. Breed Clubs also hold smaller Open Shows, where the judges are less experienced, and the social side is more informal. As there are only four Westie breed clubs in Britain, exhibitors

Show-going is an absorbing hobby, but it demands hard work and dedication.

You will need to give your Westie a last-minute grooming session before you enter the show ring.

Chalk can be applied to the coat in the run-up to a show. It forms a barrier, preventing dirt from getting into the coat. It must be removed before going into the show ring.

have to travel some distance to attend them. However, these shows are the best places to learn about Westies, and pick up tips on handling and presentation.

LOCAL OPEN AND LIMITED SHOWS
All districts have canine societies which run two shows a year. They are easy to reach, and an ideal starting place. They cater for all breeds, but entry may be very small. Here, owners learn how to show their dogs, and teach teach them about the hurly-burly of shows, without having to spend a lot of time and money on travel.

NORTH AMERICA
The American Kennel Club and the Canadian Kennel Club regulate dog shows in the USA and Canada. Shows are either All Breed Championship Shows, or Specialty Shows, which are for one breed only. Championship points can be gained at both types of show. Shows award points, according to the number of dogs of the sex and the breed present. Depending upon the location and entry, the points range from 1 to 5, and shows giving 3, 4, or 5 points are termed

'majors'. All points count towards the title Champion. In the USA to become a Champion, a dog must gain 15 points, with at least two majors under two different judges, and at least a one point win under another judge.

Classes are similar to those of Britain, but Champions enter a separate class for Best of Breed. After the Open class all the unbeaten males compete for 'Winners Dog' and it is this dog who gains the points. The same applies to the bitches, and then Winners Dog and Winners Bitch compete for Best of Winners. An award is made for Best of Opposite Sex after Best of Winners has been selected.

PREPARING TO SHOW
If you are in earnest about showing your pet Westie, take him to an experienced exhibitor, and ask him or her to give an opinion on your pet. Better still, if the breeder of your Westie has a winning kennel, go there and ask for an unbiased opinion. Ideally, you should decide whether you want to get involved in the show world *before* you buy a puppy. You can go to shows and look at the different types of Westies shown by the different kennels, and talk to the breeder whose dogs you like best. You may have to wait for a suitable puppy, as top quality show pups do not come in every litter.

While you are waiting to buy a pup, go to shows, read all you can about the breed, and spend some time in studying the Breed Standard. This is a written description of the breed, authorised by the national Kennel Club. It is a picture in words of the ideal specimen – and all judges assess entries against the Breed Standard. However, it is important to remember that the perfect dog has yet to be bred, so do not expect to find it! It is also worth bearing in mind that the idea of perfection is in the eye of the beholder, and no two people see the same picture of the perfect Westie. It is a matter of personal interpretation, which is why different dogs will win under different judges.

THE BREED STANDARD
The English Kennel Club and the American Kennel Club have much the same standard of points, although the American version has more detail. The following headings give the general outline of the ideal Westie.

GENERAL APPEARANCE
A small, hardy-looking terrier, sturdily built, with strong bone, and full of his own importance. The temperament is friendly and happy, not aggressive to humans or other dogs, but able to stand up for himself.

HEAD
The skull is slightly domed and broad. The foreface gradually tapers from the eye to the nose, which is fairly large. There is a slight indentation between the eyes, called the 'stop', and the foreface should be slightly shorter than the distance from the ear to eye.

EYES
The eyes are oval and wide apart, set deeply under bony eyebrows. The colour should be dark, and they should have a bright, intelligent expression. Light-coloured eyes or protuberant eyes are highly undesirable.

EARS
The ears are small, pointed and set erect. They are covered with smooth hair.

TEETH
Teeth are very important in any terrier breed. They should be fairly large for the size of the dog. The lower canine teeth (eye teeth) should lock in front of the upper canine teeth, and incisors or front teeth close tightly, with the top teeth over the lower teeth. The teeth should be of even size.

THE NECK
The neck is reasonably long. Writing in 1903, Colonel Malcolm said a working dog needed a reasonably long neck in order to catch and kill its prey, and this should still be bred for, even if the dog is being exhibited in the show ring. The neck should be strong and slope smoothly into the shoulders.

THE SHOULDERS
The shoulders should be well laid back and flat. The front legs are straight, with the elbows tucked well into the ribs, and covered with thick, hard hair.

THE BODY
The body is short with a level back and good depth of chest. The hindquarters are muscular and wide across the top. The hindlegs are short with a well-bent stifle. The hocks are well-set under the body when moving, in order to provide good driving action.

MOVEMENT
The movement is very important. The Westie should move strongly, with front legs swinging straight forward, and with feet pointing forward, not toeing inwards or splay-footed. The hindlegs drive the dog forward, with strength to lift the body. The overall effect is a jaunty, brisk action.

PIGMENT
The nose, lips, eye-rims and pads of the feet should be black.

TAIL
The tail is straight, carried upright. It is often described as 'carrot-shaped' – thick at the base and tapering to the tip.

COAT
The coat is very important as it is one of the most distinctive features of the

The judge assesses a class of Westies, who are being posed in the show ring.

The judge examines each Westie in turn. This is done with the dog standing on the table.

The mouth and teeth will be examined to see if the dog has the correct scissor bite, with the upper teeth closely overlapping the lower teeth.

Finally, the judge will want to see the Westie moving, in order to assess gait and overall conformation.

breed. It should consist of a straight, hard outer-coat, and a warm, soft under-coat. It should be pure white in colour.

SIZE
The Westie should measure about eleven inches (28 cms) at the withers.

SHOW TRAINING
Having decided to show your Westie, the next step is to start training him for the show ring. It is best to start when the puppy is still young, although slightly older dogs can also learn what is required

The Westie is judged when standing on a table, and so it is essential that the young puppy gets used to standing on a table right from the beginning. I find a good way to teach this is to feed the puppy every day on a firm table with a non-slip surface. The puppy should then be posed in the required show position, and have his face, mouth, feet and tail handled, so that he grows quite relaxed and happy above the floor. A few minutes a day, standing on a table and being handled, is all that is necessary at this stage.

More care should be taken with lead training than for a pet. In the show ring you want your Westie to walk smartly beside you, not too close to your feet, and with the lead slack. A dog pulling on the lead spoils his movement for the judge. When placed on the floor, the pup should learn to stand with his head held up with a tight lead, and his tail held up. He must also allow you move his feet into position, and to stand still. Again, only train for a few minutes at a time, at first. It is very important not to over-train a youngster, because a bored dog looks terrible in the ring. That is why show-training classes, held by many local dog societies, are of great benefit. Your pup can get used to other dogs, and will start to look forward to the hustle and bustle of the show ring.

PRESENTATION
Trimming for shows is a very time-consuming, and it is a skilled occupation. You will need the help of experienced exhibitors if you intend to trim your own dog. It requires daily grooming, and trimming every few days. Under no circumstances should a pet trimmer be employed, as the trimming methods for show dogs are quite different from those for pet dogs.

In addition to removing hair from the correct places, and learning to brush the hair to enhance the dog's virtues, there is the vexed problem of chalking or using some white powder to keep the coat clean. Under Kennel Club rules, powder can be used at home for trimming, but all (or as much as possible) must be removed from the coat before going to the show.

I wash my show dogs a week before a show to let the coat settle. I chalk them after drying, and then again every two days until the show. Chalk forms a barrier between the coat and any general dirt the pup might pick up during the week. This enables me to brush the hair clean. However, if the dog is to have any normal life after his first bath, the feet and face will have to be washed again the night before the show. Cleanliness in the show ring is of paramount importance. Do not forget your own appearance when you are handling in the show ring. It is important to look smart, but not over-dressed or flashy, as this will detract from your dog's appearance. Remember to wear comfortable shoes, as you will spend much of the day on your feet!

ENTERING A SHOW

Under the English system, entries for local shows should be made three or four weeks before the show, so the exhibitor must have the schedule (or flyer) in good time, and fill the form in carefully. Any mistake could lead to disqualification. In the case of the larger Championship Shows, the entries close ten to twelve weeks before the show. In the United States and Canada, entries for formal shows generally close about 18 days before a show.

On the day of the show, you must be sure to arrive in good time, and watch proceedings to see how the judge is moving the dogs, and let your dog get used to the show's noise and atmosphere.

SHOW EQUIPMENT

The equipment you will need to take to the show includes a fairly fine slip lead, a terrier pad for a final brushing of the coat, and perhaps a clip or safety pin to hold your number. You should also have basic grooming tools, a sponge and towel, and some no-rinse shampoo for last-minute cleaning up. Should you decide to progress to Championship Shows, the equipment is extensive. You would need a cage or travelling crate in which to keep the dog safe and clean at the show, a small table for preparation, water and a little food for your dog, and all the necessary grooming items such as a brush, a comb, and towels.

IN THE RING

All judges have their own ways of conducting a class, but generally, you will be asked to line up as a class, and then come forward in turn for the individual examinations. Your task is to assist the judge, when asked, so that he can examine all points of the dog. Most judges start by looking at the head. The mouth is examined to ensure the dog has the correct bite, and then the judge moves down the body, assessing forequarters, body and hindquarters. The judge will then want to see your dog move. The patterns of movement vary, but the object of the exercise is for the judge to assess movement from the front, from the rear, and in profile. When the judge reaches a decision, the successful dog and handlers are called forward. Remember to win – and lose – gracefully. If it is your lucky day, enjoy it. However, if you are unsuccessful, there is always another show and a different judge with different opinions. Most important of all, remember that this is a hobby for you and your dog, and should always be an enjoyable experience for you both. Your Westie is first and foremost a friend and a companion, and nothing changes that – no matter where you are placed in your class.

Before you decide to breed a litter, you must ensure that your bitch has a sound temperament and is free from inherited diseases.   *Anne Roslin-Williams.*

Chapter Six

BREEDING

THE RESPONSIBILITIES

Many people who know little about breeding dogs believe that a bitch – even one bought as a pet – should have at least one litter. Worse still, there is a common misconception that a bad-tempered bitch will improve in temperament after having a litter. In fact, the outcome is likely to be nasty-natured pups. Breeding a litter should only be undertaken after considerable thought, taking advice from people with experience.

Westies can be difficult whelpers, as they are a small breed but have relatively heavy bone, which sometimes makes it difficult for them to deliver the pups. It is possible to end up with no puppies, and a very expensive veterinary bill. When I was just starting to breed Westies, my first home-bred, winning bitch had to have a Caesarean, and both she and all her puppies died. When anyone suggests breeding a litter from their only pet, I remember her, and I do not think it worth the risk.

Selling puppies takes a lot of time and effort, even though our breed is popular just now. Your friends may say that they would love a puppy, but, when one is offered to them, you will find it is not as simple as that. They hope to get the pup free, or, at least, at a greatly reduced price, or they may have changed their minds, and not want one at all.

When you advertise puppies for sale, about two-thirds of the enquirers are totally unacceptable. They are either out at work all day, or have small children, or live in unsuitable accommodation. If you do not screen prospective purchasers very carefully, you may end up having to take back a puppy in poor physical condition, or one that is totally out of hand due to lack of appropriate discipline. Although you hand over responsibility for the puppy when you sell him, you cannot help but be concerned if you find out that the new owner is unable to cope satisfactorily.

MAKING THE DECISION

If you are still keen to breed a litter, and have considered all the pros and cons, the next step is to ask the breeder of your bitch for advice. The breeder will know the virtues and failings of their Westies, and will be able to confirm that your bitch is suitable to have a litter, and that she is not showing any signs of the ailments that would rule her out for breeding purposes, such as craniomandibular osteopathy (CMO), Legg-Perthes disease or slipping patellas (see Chapter Eight: Health Care).

Age is another consideration: a Westie bitch should have her first litter after about fourteen months, and before she is three years old. Younger bitches often have easier whelpings, as the muscles and bones are more flexible.

Next, you must study your bitch's pedigree in order to find a suitable stud dog. A pet dog that lives nearby, or belongs to a friend, is not advisable. An experienced stud dog should always be used, as a pet dog could damage himself or your bitch.

There are basically three options when it comes to choosing a breeding programme, which are as follows:

IN-BREEDING

This involves the closest relationship of the three systems. It is mating father to daughter, mother to son, or full brother to full sister. This close breeding should produce a very even type, as comparatively few genes are mixed.

On the other hand, characteristics which are hidden in former generations may emerge, and may not be expected. This form of breeding is risky, and should only be undertaken by very experienced breeders, and then only rarely.

LINE-BREEDING

In this type of breeding, a successful dog or bitch appears in both pedigrees. This doubling of good genes should stamp a certain number of good points, without concentrating them too much, as happens with in-breeding. This is the method used by most successful breeders, but the dog or dogs used for line-breeding must be carefully selected. A novice, who does not know the virtues and drawbacks of the dogs in earlier generations, should seek advice before pursuing this method.

OUT-CROSSING

This is when an unrelated dog and bitch are mated, or those which have no common ancestors for at least three generations. This method can produce a promising dog, but it is unlikely to produce any consistency in type in future generations. It is essential to out-cross from time to time, but again this is unlikely to be relevant for the novice breeder.

CHOOSING A STUD DOG

At this stage, you should contact the breeder and discuss which stud dog you should choose to use on your bitch. If you cannot get any assistance from your bitch's breeder, get in touch with another Westie breeder near you, who should have the knowledge of the available stud dogs, and will be able to give you advice. Be prepared to travel some distance in order to use a good stud dog. It costs as much to rear poor pups as good ones, so it cannot be stressed too strongly how important it is to go for quality – not for convenience.

It is important to contact the stud dog owner before your bitch is due in season, and to give an approximate date of when she is likely to be ready for mating. With popular and successful dogs, it is sometimes necessary to book in advance.

If possible, go and see the owner and the stud dog (take your bitch and pedigree to show the owner) to check you are happy with the dog. Even if you do not know the finer points of the breed, you must see that the dog has a nice, friendly nature. Temperament is of utmost importance in breeding, whether for pets or show stock, so a nervous or snappy dog should not be considered, however famous he is.

The owners of most Westie stud dogs are concerned for the reputation of their dogs, and will want to see your bitch and discuss the virtues and failings of their dog and your bitch. Be warned if you feel that the owner is just out to get their hands on a stud fee. If that is the case, try elsewhere.

MATING

When you have made all the arrangements, you must watch your bitch carefully for the first signs of her season (oestrous). Some bitches start with the swelling of the vulva, whereas with others the first sign is a red discharge. About ten days after the start of the discharge the colour grows paler, and the vulva is very swollen.

Contact the owner of the stud dog as soon as your bitch shows colour, and make arrangements to take your bitch. Nowadays, it is usual to take your bitch for mating on about the twelfth day after the first sign of colour. When I first started breeding dogs, we always considered the tenth day was correct. It is better to go too early, even if it means a second visit, because if you go too late, you will have to wait until the next time your bitch comes in season. If the stud dog is experienced, he will mate your bitch if she is ready.

Most pet bitches dislike it when the dog gets interested, so she will need to be held firmly. Every stud dog owner has their own method – some prefer not to have the bitch's owner present, and others need the owner to hold the bitch. If the stud dog owner asks for your help, make sure you hold your bitch firmly, and be prepared to muzzle her, if it becomes necessary.

If the stud dog owner considers that there has been a successful mating, you may feel that is sufficient, but often a second mating forty-eight hours later is advisable for a bitch being bred for the first time, especially if she has resisted the first mating. Do not leave it longer than forty-eight hours between matings, as this could lead to problems at whelping.

Although you should always be careful about the attentions of visiting dogs when your bitch is in season, you must be particularly careful after mating, as she will show much more interest in other dogs. If she gets away with a dog, there may be pups from both matings. Consult your vet if this occurs.

Westies generally make good mothers, and they will care for all their puppies' needs in the first couple of weeks after birth.

These puppies are now a week old. Their eyes will open when they are ten to fourteen days old.

At three weeks of age, the puppies are beginning to develop into individuals.

This Westie bitch is very tolerant, and even when the litter is four weeks old, she is quite happy to nurse her puppies.

PREGNANCY

The pregnancy lasts for sixty-three days or nine weeks, but you should be prepared for whelping for a week before the actual date until a week after. Your bitch should be kept on her normal diet, with her normal amount of exercise, for the first five weeks after mating, then she can have some extra rations.

I give my bitches 3 ozs lean, raw, chopped beef at lunchtime, with their ration of dry biscuits, and I add a little calcium, with Vitamin D supplement, to the evening meal. There are several different calcium additives which you can get from the pet shop, or you can ask your vet for advice.

In the sixth week after mating, there are usually signs that the bitch is in whelp. The teats become very pink in colour and are slightly swollen, and if you feel your bitch's abdomen very gently after a meal, it will probably feel tight.

Some people may advocate worming your bitch while she is pregnant, but I do not like giving anything to a pregnant bitch. You should check that your bitch's inoculation and worming programmes are up-to-date before you mate her. If your bitch gets very heavy in late pregnancy, her meals should be divided into three, and her exercise should be carefully supervised. Regular exercise should be maintained, but do not allow the bitch too much activity. Car journeys should be avoided in the last two weeks.

It is important to groom your bitch more carefully than usual at this time. The long hair around her hind end and underneath should be kept short for purposes of hygiene. During pregnancy you must watch for any vaginal discharge. There is always a clear, sticky discharge when a bitch is in whelp, but any coloured discharge, red, brown or green, usually spells serious trouble, and your vet should be consulted at once.

PREPARATIONS FOR WHELPING

When you are certain your bitch is in whelp, or even if you are not too sure, you should be making preparations for her whelping accommodation. Ideally, you should use a good-quality wooden box, with a gap in one side, so that the bitch can get in and out easily. The top should be open, so that you can get a good view of the proceedings.

The box should be in a room which you can keep warm, and one that is quiet – away from the hurly-burly of the household. It is generally advisable to keep the temperature of the room at 70 degrees Fahrenheit. You can use an infra-red lamp, which must be at least four feet above the box, or one of the specially heated pads that are available now.

I use infra-red lamps, as some of my bitches dig up their bedding very vigorously, and I am nervous of having a source of heat within their reach. The best bedding is plenty of newspapers, placed in the bed in layers, about half an inch thick.

This is warm, dry and easily changed. You should also have sterilised scissors, cotton-wool (cotton), old face cloths or pieces of towel (scrupulously clean), and some disinfectant handy.

WHELPING
Most bitches whelp a day or two before the expected day, or a day late. Have a word with the vet, if your bitch is more than two days late, but if she is behaving normally, and has no discharge, you will probably be advised to wait a little longer before thinking of veterinary intervention.

Prior to whelping, the bitch will usually go to her bed, or to the new whelping box, and dig up the bedding. Keep an eye on her during the few days before she is due to whelp, as Westies do like to find their own place, and it is likely to be under the garden shed, or somewhere equally impractical.

The digging phase is followed by panting and trembling. The bitch's temperature will drop from 101 degrees Fahrenheit to 98 degrees Fahrenheit, and the vulva will be enlarged. The next stage, which can start almost immediately or take some hours, will be the onset of contractions, and clear fluid will be discharged as the water bag bursts. The contractions will increase, and your bitch will probably want to walk about. With each contraction, she will arch her back and push strongly. The puppy will appear at the mouth of the vulva, and with a few more contractions, the puppy will be expelled.

Pick up the puppy immediately, using a piece of towel, and remove the membrane that covers the puppy's head, and wipe the mucous from his nose. The placenta or afterbirth attached to the pup by the umbilical cord may have come with the pup, or the cord may have broken, leaving the placenta in the bitch. In either case, cut the cord about an inch from the puppy, using your sterilised scissors, and rub the puppy firmly until you are sure that he is breathing properly. Hold the pup with his head hanging down, and open his mouth carefully with your little finger to help clear the fluid from his lungs.

If the afterbirth is not expelled with the puppy, it may come before the next puppy, or the bitch may retain it for some time. If she wishes to eat the afterbirth when she expels it, let her do so, as it contains many valuable nutrients. Keep a count of the afterbirths, so that you can tell the vet whether or not all have been accounted for.

If your bitch strains strongly for an hour or so, with no result, you must call the vet, in case there is a misplaced puppy. If a puppy gets stuck when it is partially out, get a firm grip on him, using a piece of towel to hold the body, as it is very slippery. As the bitch strains, pull the pup out and downwards. The direction is very important. If you cannot get a grip on the puppy, leave it until your vet can see your bitch. Do not start doing internal investigations of any sort, as you could easily do considerable damage.

When the whelping is over, ask your vet to check that all is well. He will probably give the bitch an injection to clear out any bits of the placenta. While the vet is with you, ask him to inspect the puppies, especially looking for cleft palates, which occasionally occur in Westies.

These puppies are now fully weaned and are eating cereal from a dish.

An outdoor pen is ideal as the litter gets older, as long as the puppies also have access to a larger area to play in. Shade and bedding should be provided.

The puppies will enjoy having toys, but make sure they are totally safe.

Westies are
notoriously
inquisitive,
and the
growing
puppies will
be keen to
explore their
surroundings

CARING FOR THE NURSING BITCH

A nursing bitch needs peace and quiet. I believe in handling each puppy in turn once a day to see that they are all well, but no-one else should touch them. Your bitch must be taken out at regular intervals, as no bitch will dirty her kennel, unless she is desperate, and this is particularly important for a house dog.

Needless to say, food must be of good nutritional value, but it should not be too rich. My nursing bitches are given a light diet for three days. This consists of four feeds a day, mainly composed of milk pudding, egg and milk. If your bitch does not like too much milk, she should be given chicken. After three days, I give four meals daily, two consisting of milk pudding, and two of meat and biscuit.

REARING THE LITTER

If the pups cry continuously and are not sucking, you will have to try to teach them to suck by opening their mouths and attaching them to a teat. You must use your judgement as to how much interference your bitch will tolerate, as upsetting your bitch will make matters worse.

As a last resort, you will have to feed the pups with a special milk which you can obtain from your vet. Small feeding bottles are available, but, at first, you will do better with a medicine dropper, which enables you to drop the milk into the puppy's mouth, very carefully, a drop at a time. All things being equal, the bitch will feed and clean the pups for the first three weeks, and then you should take over.

The bitch and puppies should be kept warm, but not too hot. The best type of bedding is the fleecy imitation sheepskin, which makes a warm and comfortable bed, and is easy to clean. However, it is safer to use newspaper for the first week or so, if your bitch digs up the bedding.

At three weeks, you can offer the pups a little warm milk, and if they seem interested in it, you should feed them twice a day. Between three and four weeks, the puppies should be given some good-quality, raw meat, scraped or very finely minced. You should start with very small quantities, and increase as the puppies grow. By the time they are four and a half weeks old, the pups will be eating four meals a day, two of milk and cereal, and two of chopped meat.

Worming can be carried out at four weeks or after. You can obtain a suitable liquid wormer or tablets from your vet. From this point onwards, during the next four weeks, the puppies will grow very quickly. Their food should be increased, and they should be given a variety of foods – cooked and canned meat, and different cereals with their milk – so that they are prepared for changes, when, at approximately nine weeks old, they are ready to go to their new homes.

Chapter Seven

HEALTH CARE

FINDING A VETERINARIAN

Carefully-bred and well-reared Westies are usually extremely healthy, and should be infrequent visitors to the veterinary surgeon. Nevertheless, it is important to have contact with a veterinary practice which is readily accessible in times of emergency, and also where you like and trust the veterinary surgeons.

Your first meeting with the vet will probably be when you take your new puppy for his first inoculation. The vet will check the puppy for any ailments before injecting him. You will need to note carefully how the vet handles your puppy, making sure that the pup is not frightened in any way, but is held gently and firmly. If your puppy behaves badly, screams or attempts to bite, you must assess honestly whether it is because the vet is too rough with him or because your own attitude is too protective. Do not hesitate to go to another practice if you feel that the vet is at fault. Some vets do not like or have little interest in small animals, and may be unintentionally heavy-handed.

With luck and good management, the annual trip to the vet for inoculation boosters will be the only time you go. However, you must feel that your contact with the vet is secure enough to enable you to ask his advice as soon as anything goes wrong.

ASSESSING CONDITION

When you know your dog well, you will soon be able to tell whether there is something seriously wrong with him, or if he is just a little under the weather. Quite often, dogs will refuse a meal. Do not immediately offer something tastier or richer, as this will only serve to aggravate an upset stomach. Instead, fast the dog for twenty-four hours before offering more food. However, you must make sure that fresh drinking water is available.

A dog can vomit food quite readily, but if there is blood present, or the dog drinks copiously and vomits the water, you should consult your vet.

COMMON AILMENTS

ABSCESSES (INTERDIGITAL CYSTS): Some Westies are prone to cysts between the toes. The first symptom is limping, or carrying one foot. Then, in a day or two, the foot swells between the toes and feels very hot. There does not seem to be a known cause, but once the abscess has burst, the pain goes. The best course of action is to soak the foot in water as hot as the dog can stand (usually a little cooler than your hand can stand), with a spoonful of salt in the water. Do this several times daily until the abscess bursts, and then the dog will keep it clean by licking it.

ANAL GLANDS: The anal glands are situated on either side of the anus. Their original use was for scent marking, and they still give off a distinctive smell, especially if the dog is frightened. Normally, these glands are kept clean by defecation, but if the motions are too loose, the glands fail to get the necessary pressure to clear them. The signs are an unpleasant smell, and the dog drags his rear along the floor or chews around his tail in order to relieve the irritation. An abscess will occur if the glands are not emptied, so visit the vet.

ARTHRITIS: This is something that affects older dogs. The veteran Westie will tolerate stiffness, but, if your dog appears to be in pain, a half aspirin will help. Cod-liver oil is reputed to be beneficial, but do not over-do the dosage.

BURNS AND SCALDS: The treatment for burns and scalds is the same as that for humans. Rinse the affected area under a cold tap in order to take the heat out, and cut away as much hair as possible. In minor cases, apply a soothing ointment; in more severe cases, professional help must be sought. The badly-burned dog will be suffering from shock, and should be kept warm and quiet in his bed or crate.

CANKER: This term was used for many years to cover any ear problem. Nowadays, there are many different treatments for the different causes. The first symptom of an ear problem is the dog scratching or rubbing an ear, holding the ear down, and sometimes even holding the whole head askew. Very often, there is also an unpleasant smell. As there are so many different lotions on the market, it is best to get a treatment from your vet. If drops are applied, as directed, for a week, and there is no improvement, go back to the vet for a change of medication. Do not keep on for months with drops that are not clearing the condition, as this will lead to a chronic infection.

CAR SICKNESS: Most pups are sick when first introduced to the car. Your puppy should be trained by being taken for short rides, either firmly settled on someone's knee (duly prepared with towels etc.), or in a crate to prevent him from moving around the car. If each journey ends with a short, enjoyable walk, the pup will connect the car with pleasure. By taking trouble of this kind, most dogs will grow out of this problem. Quite often, you will find that there are certain places in the car where your dog will settle best. Car sickness tablets are available, but they can cause drowsiness, so it is not advisable to use them if going to a show or even for a day out. However, herbal tablets can be effective. No food should be given to your Westie for a couple of hours before travelling, and he should be allowed to relieve himself before you start.

CONSTIPATION: If this occurs frequently, it is usually caused by incorrect feeding. Bones can severely upset some dogs, and, if this is the case, they should not be fed. A change of exercising time can also cause problems, as dogs are very much creatures of habit, and if they have to wait too long to pass a motion, problems can arise. The best treatment is a teaspoonful of liquid paraffin. If constipation persists, change the diet or consult your vet. Sometimes, when a dog is constipated or has diarrhoea, he passes a drop or two of blood. As long as it is only a trace, it will pass; but, if there is a fair amount, it should be treated seriously.

DIARRHOEA: This is a very common warning sign for more serious troubles, and should always be investigated. Change of diet is the most common cause, so, if your dog does not seem unwell, but has eaten something unsuitable, fast him for twenty-four hours, and offer water or water with glucose. This should clear it up. Do not give milk, as this will increase the diarrhoea.

If the condition persists, professional help must be sought. So many problems start with diarrhoea, such as: gastro-enteritis, parvovirus, foreign bodies in the gut or worm infestation. Stress can also cause this condition. If you know your dog, you will know when he has been under stress.

Diarrhoea should not be allowed to drag on for many days, as the dog will become dehydrated, and will become more seriously ill.

FITS: The cause of fits are many and varied, but, fortunately, they are not very common in our breed. Puppies may have an occasional fit because of over-excitement, or when teething. The signs are that the pup will fall over, may froth at the mouth, and his legs will twitch. If this happens, the dog should be held firmly, with a cold, damp cloth placed over his eyes, until he regains consciousness. Keep the dog quiet for a couple of hours, and if there is a recurrence, seek professional help.

LAMENESS: There are many reasons for lameness. Interdigital cysts (see Abscesses) often cannot be seen for a day or so. If your Westie appears to be lame, check the pads for thorns, cracks, or a small stone or dried mud wedged between the pads. If you find evidence of any of these things, bathe the affected foot in warm, soapy water. Next, check the toenails. If one is painful, the dog may have knocked it and bruised it, or even pulled it off.

If the nail has been pulled out of position, bathe with a mild antiseptic and use an antiseptic cream. Care must be taken that the toe does not become infected. If this does happen, your dog will need a course of antibiotics.

If the foot does not appear to be the source of the trouble, gently feel up the leg, moving it back and forward. A day or two's rest should improve a mild sprain, but, if the pain continues, a visit to the vet will be necessary.

PHANTOM PREGNANCY: Some bitches are very prone to phantom pregnancies. About seven weeks after the end of her season, the bitch will become quiet, may refuse food, and will start digging up her bed, or trying to make a nest in an out-of-the-way place. She may collect up small toys and guard them like new-borns. Some bitches also produce milk. If the mammary glands become over-full with milk and feel hard, medication will be needed to reduce the milk. In most cases, there is not enough milk to cause a problem. Your bitch should be encouraged to go for walks, and taken out in the car. Keep the toys out of her reach, and she will return to normal in a week or so.

STINGS: Dogs are very inclined to snap at bees or wasps, and this should be severely discouraged. If a dog is stung in the mouth, antihistamine injections are vital, so you will need to see your vet immediately. Stings on the body should be treated as with humans. Remove the sting of a bee, if visible. Bathe with vinegar and water for wasps; bicarbonate of soda for bees.

PARASITES (INTERNAL)
There are two types of worm that most commonly affect dogs. They are:
Roundworms (Toxocara canis): This is the worm that the media makes much of, as, in rare cases, it can cause blindness in children, if they happen to eat the eggs of the worms.All dogs should be regularly dosed for roundworms. Although roundworms are often called 'puppy' worms, they also occur in adult dogs, and they should be treated accordingly. Wormers can be administered to puppies as young as three weeks old. Some vets recommend frequent treatments, but I have known Westies who have ended up with permanent stomach problems from too many treatments. I worm my pups two or three times before nine weeks, depending on whether or not the pup produces many worms. After that, I worm at sixteen weeks, and not again until seven months. There are many different worming remedies, and they come in the form of pills, syrup or granules.
Tapeworms: These do not usually affect puppies, and I have only rarely found them in my dogs. The dog is infected by eating the larvae from a dead rabbit, or, more frequently, the intermediate host is a flea. The dog loses condition, but the presence of tapeworm segments around the dog's anus is the clearest symptom. The segments look like small grains of rice, and can also be seen in the faeces. Once again, there are many pills that can be used to clear up this condition.

EXTERNAL
FLEAS: Fleas are a common parasite, and they flourish in warm houses with wall to wall carpeting. The fleas live in the carpet, and go to the dog or cat to feed. The first signs are usually small, black, grit-like particles in the dog's coat,

commonly called flea dirt. The fleas are dark brown, and move very quickly through the dog's coat. The treatment can vary from flea powder to medicated washes and aerosol spray. Follow the instructions carefully, as over-dosing with some of the modern flea controls can be dangerous to the dog. Bedding and sleeping quarters should be thoroughly washed in order to get rid of any eggs.

LICE: These are small off-white insects which attach themselves to the dog. They do not run as fleas do. Their eggs or nits are laid in the dog's coat, and appear like scurf. The dog can scratch and create bald patches. The treatment is to bathe the dog in an intsecticidal shampoo, obtained from the vet or a pet shop. Care should be taken with young pups, as many modern preparations cannot be used on puppies. It is, therefore, important to make sure your bitch is clear of all mites before mating.

TICKS: Ticks are usually picked up on country walks. They vary in size, depending on whether they come from a sheep or a rabbit. The tick buries its head in the dog's skin and sucks the blood. Eventually, the tick will fall off, leaving a nasty sore that may go septic. Care should be taken when removing ticks. A piece of cotton-wool (cotton), soaked in methylated spirits or surgical spirits, should be placed over the tick, and after a few seconds the tick can be pulled off. If the tick is near the eye where spirits cannot be used, cover the tick with Vaseline instead. Some antiseptic ointment should be applied, and care must be taken to ensure that an abscess does not form on the wound.

HARVEST MITES: These are very small, orange mites, which occur in some country areas, and are unheard of in others. They appear between the middle of July and the end of September. Many dogs have harvest mites in their coats without any problems resulting, but some are badly affected. Benzyl Benzoate is the best remedy. Rub this well into the skin, especially into the toes.

BREED ASSOCIATED CONDITIONS
CRANIOMANDIBULAR OSTEOPATHY (CMO): This is an inherited disease, but the inheritance pattern is not clear. The condition is a non-cancerous growth of bone, usually on the jaw-bone, but occasionally on other bones. The first symptoms are difficulty in eating or pain when the mouth is opened. It can start at four weeks of age until about ten months, but more often it occurs between four and seven months. It is treated with anti-inflammatory drugs, and is almost always curable. Dogs that have developed the condition should not be used for breeding.

KERATOCONJUNCTIVITIS SICCA (DRY EYE): This is a condition of the eyes which is caused by reduced tear production, making the eyeball dry because of lack of moisture for lubrication. It is a painful condition which usually occurs in middle age. It is now thought to arise from an auto-immune condition, but there is much more research needed to confirm this. Many notable breeders, of many years standing, have seen very few cases, but the veterinary profession says that many Westies are affected. As yet, there is no proof of heredity.

LEGG-PERTHES DISEASE: As yet, there is no proof of this condition being inherited, but it occurs in many small breeds. The condition affects the hip, and, as far as it is known, is caused by a knock or a twist to the hind leg. This can cut off the blood supply to the head of the femur, making the bone crumble. It occurs between the ages of four and eleven months. The first symptom is slight lameness in the hind leg. The leg causes the dog progressively more pain, and there is a noticeable loss of muscle in the hindquarter. It can occur in one or both hindlegs. One treatment is to surgically remove the head of the femur, which reduces the pain, and the muscle builds up again. On the other hand, less severe cases can be left to build up muscle without removing any bone. The operation usually speeds up recovery. In most cases, the dog regains almost total movement in the leg. Although there is no proof of heredity, it is unwise to use affected dogs for breeding.

SLIPPING PATELLA: The patella is the knee or stifle joint, which is held in place by ligaments. In some dogs, the ligaments are too long, allowing the knee to slip out of place. In more cases, it is just loose, but can cause pain. It may be necessary to have the leg operated on. In Westies, there is no definite pattern of inheritance, but severe cases should not be bred from.

SKIN PROBLEMS: Many vets say that Westies are prone to skin trouble. Some of these problems may be inherited, but many of the skin conditions in the breed are caused by the modern environment. Houses are very warm in winter when the Westie has a thick coat; the dog gets over-heated and starts scratching. Then the lesions get infected and become septic. The cure is a course of antibiotics, but the dog should not be allowed to get too warm, and the coat should be kept trimmed. Other skin problems can be traced to the type of cleaning preparations used on bedding and towels (if possible, use soap or non-biological powders), insufficient or incorrect groming, and, more than anything else, incorrect feeding. Westies do best without too much rich food. Too many additives and too much protein are sources of trouble. Westies should not be allowed to become too fat. They need plenty of fresh air and exercise to keep the skin supple.

SUMMARY

We are fortunate that the Westie is a hardy little dog, and, with luck, you should enjoy many years of happy companionship. The key is vigilance: keep a close check on your Westie, and you will spot the first sign of trouble before it has a chance to develop into a problem.